# The EU Killed My Dad

## Aaron Kilercioglu

T0023960

*methuen* | drama

LONDON · NEW YORK · OXFORD · NEW DELHI · SYDNEY

METHUEN DRAMA
Bloomsbury Publishing Plc
50 Bedford Square, London, WC1B 3DP, UK
1385 Broadway, New York, NY 10018, USA
29 Earlsfort Terrace, Dublin 2, Ireland

BLOOMSBURY, METHUEN DRAMA and the Methuen
Drama logo are trademarks of Bloomsbury Publishing Plc

First published in Great Britain 2024

Cover image design by Ciaran Walsh (CIWA Design)

This text went to press prior to the first production,
and may not reflect the final script.

A catalogue record for this book is available from the British Library.

Library of Congress Control Number: 2023952494.

ISBN: PB: 978-1-3504-6301-1
ePDF: 978-1-3504-6302-8
eBook: 978-1-3504-6303-5

Series: Modern Plays

Typeset by Mark Heslington Ltd, Scarborough, North Yorkshire

To find out more about our authors and books visit
www.bloomsbury.com and sign up for our newsletters.

# Woven Voices Prize

The Woven Voices Prize for Playwriting platforms the voices of migrant playwrights in the UK.

Run by Woven Voices and Jermyn Street Theatre, the Prize seeks to promote a multicultural Britain and to champion migrant voices in the theatre industry. Each year, the winning play is produced at Jermyn Street Theatre, the West End's studio theatre.

As of 2024, two Woven Voice Prize winners have been selected.

Kazakhstan-born writer Karina Wiedman was the inaugural winner of the prize with *The Anarchist* in 2022. Wiedman's critically acclaimed play was nominated for the Off West End Awards in the categories Best Director and Best Ensemble.

In 2023, Austrian-born, Turkish/Canadian writer and director Aaron Kilercioglu won the prize for his play *The EU Killed My Dad*.

Further information at
**www.wovenvoicesprize.co.uk**

Photography of *The Anarchist* by Steve Gregson.

# The West End's Studio Theatre at 30

Jermyn Street Theatre is a unique 70-seat theatre in Piccadilly Circus. World-class, household-name playwrights, directors and theatrical legends like Siân Phillips and Trevor Nunn work here alongside those taking their first steps in professional theatre. It is a crucible for multigenerational talent.

We stage world premieres, rare revivals and reimagined classics, and collaborate with theatres across the world. Our productions have transferred across the UK, to Broadway and beyond.

30 years ago in 1994, Howard Jameson and Penny Horner (who continue to serve as Chair of the Board and Executive Director today) created the theatre out of what had been the staff changing room for the restaurant upstairs with no core funding. Since then, the theatre has flourished thanks to a mixture of earned income from box office sales and the generosity of individual patrons and trusts and foundations. In 2017, the theatre became a full-time producing house. We won the Stage Award for Fringe Theatre of the Year in both 2012 and 2021.

Caroline Quentin in *Infamous*.
Photography by Steve Gregson.

Archie Backhouse, Forbes Masson and Daniel Boyd in *Farm Hall*. Photography by Alex Brenner.

**JERMYN STREET THEATRE 30**

# Support Us *at* 30

Wondering what to get us for our big birthday? Your Friendship makes the best present of all!

Over the last 30 years, we've made a name for ourselves as the West End's Studio theatre. With just 70 seats, **our small scale is our greatest strength**: a unique place where artists can afford to take risks and audiences can afford to see the work.

But even with every seat filled, **ticket sales only generate 60%** of what we need to build our productions, fund our small team, and champion the next generation of artists. We rely on the generosity of donors like you for the remaining 40%. **Your support ensures we can build on the legacy of the last three decades** and make the next 30 years the most exciting yet.

## Lifeboat Friends

(From £4.50 a month)

Our **Lifeboat Friends** are the heart of Jermyn Street Theatre. Benefits include
- Dedicated Priority Booking period.
- Invitation to a Friends Night for each production, with a chance to meet the cast.

## The Miranda Club

(From £45 a month)

Members of **The Miranda Club** enjoy all the benefits of the Ariel club, plus
- Acknowledgement in our Front of House.
- Annual Friends Lunch with our Artistic Director.
- Invitation to one Press Night/Gala Night per year.
- Behind-the-scenes access and a closer relationship with our team.

## The Ariel Club

(From £12.50 a month)

**Ariel Club** members receive all the benefits of Lifeboat Friends, plus:
- Chances to attend Press Nights.
- Complimentary signed programme or playtext for each production.
- Acknowledgement in programmes, playtexts, and on our website.

## The Director's Circle

(From £250 a month)

The **Director's Circle** is an inner circle of our most generous donors. They are invited to every Press Night and enjoy regular informal contact with our Artistic Director and team. The fir t to hear our plans they often act as a valuable sounding board.

To join us, visit, www.jermynstreettheatre.co.uk/friends/
Jermyn Street Theatre is a Registered Charity No. 1186940

# Our Friends

## The Ariel Club

Richard Alexander
David Barnard
Derek Baum
Martin Bishop
Dmitry Bosky
Katie Bradford
Nigel Britten
Christopher Brown
Donald Campbell
James Carroll
Ted Craig
Jeanette Culver
Shomit Dutta
Jill & Paul Dymock
Lucy Fleming
Anthony Gabriel
Carol Gallagher
Roger Gaynham
Paul Guinery
Debbie Guthrie
Diana Halfnight
Julie Harries
Eleanor Harvey
Andrew Hughes
Mark Jones
Margaret Karliner
David Lanch
Caroline Latham
Isabelle Laurent
Christine MacCallum
Keith Macdonald
Vivien Macmillan-Smith
Nicky Oliver
Sally Padovan
Kate & John Peck
Adrian Platt
Alexander Powell
Oliver Prenn
Martin Sanderson

Carolyn Shapiro
Nigel Silby
Philip Somervail
Robert Swift
Gary Trimby
George Warren
Lavinia Webb
Ann White
Ian Williams
John Wise
George Warren
Lavinia Webb
Ann White
Ian Williams
John Wise

## The Miranda Club

Anonymous
Anthony Ashplant
Gyles & Michèle Brandreth
Sylvia de Bertodano
Robyn Durie
Richard Edgecliffe-Johnson
Maureen Elton
Nora Franglen
Mary Godwin
Louise Greenberg
Ros & Alan Haigh
Phyllis Huvos
Marta Kinally
Yvonne Koenig
Hilary Lemaire
Jane Mennie
Charles Paine
John & Terry Pearson
Iain Reid
Ros Shelley
Martin Shenfiel
Carol Shephard-Blandy

Jenny Sheridan
Sir Bernard Silverman
Brian Smith
Frank Southern
Mark Tantam
Paul Taylor
Geraldine Terry
Brian & Esme Tyers

## Director's Circle

Anonymous
Philip Carne MBE &
   Christine Carne
Jocelyn Abbey & Tom Carney
Colin Clark RIP
Lynette & Robert Craig
Gary Fethke
Flora Fraser
Robert & Pirjo Gardiner
Charles Glanville &
   James Hogan
Crawford & Mary Harris
Ros & Duncan McMillan
Leslie & Peter
   MacLeod-Miller
James L. Simon
Peter Soros & Electra Toub
Fiona Stone
Melanie Vere Nicoll
Robert Westlake &
   Marit Mohn

# The EU Killed My Dad

Performed at the Jermyn Street Theatre, London from 23 January to 6 February 2024 with the following cast:

## Cast

| | |
|---|---|
| Mustafa + Investigator 2 | TIRAN AAKEL |
| Umut + others | OJAN GENC |
| Bahriye / Janice + others | ROSIE HILAL |
| Berker | LUCA KAMLEH CHAPMAN |
| Elif | DILEK ŞENGÜL |

## Production Team

| | |
|---|---|
| Writer | AARON KILERCIOGLU |
| Director | GEORGIA GREEN |
| Designer | CORY SHIPP |
| Lighting Designer | LUCÍA SÁNCHEZ ROLDÁN |
| Sound Designer | JASMIN KENT RODGMAN |
| Movement Director | ADI GORTLER |
| | |
| Production Manager | LUCY MEWIS-McKERROW |
| Stage Manager | JAMIE KIBISCH-WILES |
| | |
| Executive Producer | DAVID DOYLE |
| Producer | GABRIELE UBOLDI |

Special thanks to Global Voices Theatre and the readers for the Woven Voices Prize.

# Tiran Aakel

## Mustafa + Investigator 2

Theatre includes: *The Girl on the Train* (Salisbury Playhouse); *The Mother of Kamal* (Camden Festival); *The Best Exotic Marigold Hotel* (No 1 tour); *The Kite Runner* (UK/Dubai tour); *The Jungle* (Playhouse Theatre, West End); *Umm Kalthoum and The Golden Era* (Dubai Opera House); *Our White Skoda Octavia* (Eastern Angles); *Blueprint Medea* (Finborough Theatre); *Burkas and Bacon Butties* (VAULT Festival); *I Was Looking at the Ceiling and Then I Saw the Sky* (UK tour).

Television includes: *Eastenders*, *Casualty* (BBC); *The Bill* (ITV).

Tiran trained at East 15 Acting School.

# Ojan Genc

## Umut + others

Previously for Jermyn Street Theatre: *The Anarchist*.

Theatre includes: *Trade* (The Pleasance Theatre).

Television includes: *Slow Horses, Silo* (Apple TV); *Industry S3* (BBC).

Ojan trained at Drama Centre, London.

# Rosie Hilal

## Bahriye / Janice + others

Theatre includes: *Unexpected Twist* (Royal & Derngate/Fiery Angel); *Harry Potter and the Cursed Child* (Palace Theatre); *Becoming Berenice* (Forge/Voila Europe); *Macbeth* (Stafford Shakespeare); *Brideshead Revisited* (ETT/York Theatre Royal); *The Hard Problem* (The National Theatre); *The Oresteia*, *Measure for Measure*, *Anthony and Cleopatra*, *Holy Warriors* (Shakespeare's Globe); *The Hypochondriac* (Globe, Wanamaker Theatre); *All's Well That Ends Well*, *As You Like It/Hamlet* (Royal Shakespeare Company); *Occupied* (Theatre 503).

Film includes: *North Star* (CAA Media); *London Road* (BBC/National Theatre).

Television includes: *Disclaimer* (Apple TV+); *All the Light We Cannot See* (Netflix); *No Return* (ITV1).

Radio/voice work includes: *The Street* (Nico Muhly/King's College Cambridge); *Andromache, Figleaf* (BBC Radio 4).

## Luca Kamleh Chapman
### Berker

Theatre includes: *Grey Rock* (Remote Theatre Project); *two Palestinians go dogging* (Royal Court Theatre); *A Lie of the Mind, A Couple of Poor, Polish-Speaking Romani, As You Like It, Medea* (Oxford School of Drama).

Film includes: *Anna* (Good Films Collective); *How to Have Sex* (Film 4/BFI).

Television includes: *The Gathering* (Channel 4/World Productions).

## Dilek Şengül
### Elif

Theatre includes: *Reasons to Stay Alive, Othello* (English Touring Theatre); *Contractions* (Trafalgar Studios); *Cuzco* (Theatre503); *Octopus* (Greenwich Theatre); *The Wild Party* (Tobacco Factory).

Television includes: *No Return* (ITV); *MotherFatherSon* (BBC); *Eastenders* (BBC).

Film includes: *The Barber* (Film4/BFI Network); *Snake Pit* (Two Birds Entertainment); *Addi & Chess* (Two Birds Entertainment); *The Chocolate Wrapper* (Elijah Productions).

Dilek trained at Bristol Old Vic Theatre School.

# Aaron Kilercioglu

## Writer

Theatre includes: *For A Palestinian* (Bristol Old Vic/Camden People's Theatre); *A Guest* (Vault Festival); *CICADA 3301* (Underbelly)

Film includes: *100 Days Since* (Short Film); *Abteil 4* (Short Film)

Aaron is a writer and director currently under commission writing his debut feature film for Karga7, an original play for Eleanor Lloyd Company, and a musical adaptation for Zorlu PSM, Istanbul. His past work includes the critically acclaimed, sell-out hit *For A Palestinian*. A member of writers groups at the Old Vic, London Library, and Bush Theatre, his work was shortlisted for the Theatre 503 International Playwriting Prize. He has won the Woven Voices Prize, the BOLD Playwrights Prize, and the Methuen Drama prize.

# Georgia Green

## Director

Theatre (as Director) includes: *Invisible* (59e59, New York City/Bush Theatre); *Gloria* (RADA); *Ruckus* (Southwark Playhouse/Edinburgh Summerhall/UK tour 2024); *Pilgrims* (Guildhall School of Music and Drama); *Three Sisters, Blue Stockings, You Got Older* (LAMDA); *Human Animals* (Royal Welsh College of Music and Drama); *Twelfth Night* (ALRA); *Parliament Square* (Rose Bruford); *OUTSIDE: Three new plays by Kalungi Ssebandeke, Sonali Bhattacharyya and Zoe Cooper, The Mikvah Project* (Orange Tree Theatre).

Theatre (as Staff/Assistant/Associate Director) includes: *Infinite Life* (National Theatre); *Emilia* (LAMDA); *Dirty Crusty* (Yard Theatre); *Amsterdam* (ATC/Orange Tree Theatre/Theatre Royal Plymouth); *Out of Water, The Double Dealer* (Orange Tree Theatre); *Zog* (Rose Theatre Kingston/Freckle Productions/Kneehigh); Tiddler (Freckle Productions).

Radio includes: *The Get* (BBC Radio 3); *The Mikvah Project* (BBC Radio 4).

Georgia Green is a director and writer who trained at the Orange Tree Theatre. She was recently Resident Director at the National

Theatre Studio. She has been a lead facilitator at Cardboard Citizens, a mentor on the MFA Playwriting at Central School of Speech and Drama and has been a reader for the Bruntwood Prize and Orange Tree Theatre. She has taught on the MFA in Directing and Acting at LAMDA.

## Cory Shipp

### Designer

Theatre (as Designer) includes: *The Mikvah Project* (Orange Tree Theatre); *Hansel & Gretel* (Chiswick Playhouse); *Cyrano de Bergerac, Easy Virtue* (The Watermill Theatre); *Mr Burns: A Post-Electric Play, RENT, Return to the Forbidden Planet, Vinegar Tom* (Mountview Theatre Academy); *Another Planet* (The Gramophones Theatre Company); *Justice in a Day* (Theatr Clwyd); *Hags* (Scratchworks Theatre Company); *Boy, Blue Stockings, Tristan and Yseult, Much Ado about Nothing* (LAMDA); *Cinderella* (The Barn Theatre); *Pilgrims* (Guildhall); *Spring Awakening, Merrily We Roll Along, Spongebob the Musical, Company* (Leeds Conservatoire); *Anyone Can Whistle* (Southwark Playhouse).

Theatre (as Costume Designer) includes: *Unfortunate: A Musical Parody* (Fat Rascal Theatre Company/Underbelly Festival); *Bandstand, Sweeney Todd* (ArtsEd).

Theatre (as Set Designer) includes: *Wipe These Tears* (Bezna Theatre Company); *Justice in a Day* (Theatr Clwyd); *Sweet Charity* (ArtsEd); *The Lion, The B!tch and The Wardrobe* (Wales Millennium Centre).

Cory is a set and costume designer working across all ranges of performative work across the UK. Cory trained at the Royal Welsh College of Music and Drama.

*coryshippdesign.com*

## Lucía Sánchez Roldán

### Lighting Designer

Theatre (as Lighting Designer) includes: *Under Milk Wood* (Sherman Theatre); *Papercut* (Park 90); *How to Succeed in Business Without Really Trying* (Southwark Playhouse Large); *Orpheus Descending*

(National Theatre of Albania); *We'll Be Who We Are* (RnD Vaults); *The Walworth Farce* (Southwark Playhouse Elephant); *Wonderful World of Dissocia* (Stratford East); *Grate* (National Theatre of Kosovo); *Fefu and Her Friends, Not about Nightingales* (Tobacco Factory); *Bogeyman* (Pleasance/Camden's People Theatre); *Black, el Payaso* (Arcola Theatre/Cervantes Theatre); *Camp Albion* (Watermill Theatre); *We Are the Best!* (Live Theatre); *Tapped* (Theatre 503); *The Forest Awakens, Code and Dagger, A New Beginning* (Kiln Theatre); *The Gift* (GBS RADA); *Barbarians* (Silk Street); *Everything Must Go* (The Playground Theatre); *Invisibles, The First* (VAULT Festival); *The Spirit* (BAC); *Ms Julie, Utopia Room* (The Place); *The Niceties* (Finborough Theatre); *How We Begin* (Kings Head Theatre).

Theatre (as Co-Lighting Designer) includes: *Suddenly, Last Summer* (English Theatre Frankfurt).

Theatre (as Associate Lighting Designer) includes: *Stranger Things: The First Shadow* (Phoenix Theatre); *Drive Your Plow Over the Bones of the Dead* (Complicité); *two Palestinians go dogging* (Royal Court Theatre); *Cabaret* (Playhouse); *Camp Siegfried* (Old Vic); *Taboo Anniversary Concert* (London Palladium); *The Mirror and the Light* (Gielgud Theatre); *Amélie* (Criterion Theatre); *Les Misérables – The Staged Concert* (Sondheim Theatre); *Moonlight and Magnolias* (Nottingham Playhouse); *The Fishermen* (West End/Marlowe Theatre).

# Jasmin Kent Rodgman

## Composer and Sound Designer

Theatre includes: *Julius Caesar* (Royal Shakespeare Company); *Titus Andronicus* (Shakespeare's Globe); *Paradise Now, Harm* (Bush Theatre); *Brown Girls Do It Too* (Soho Theatre); *Britannicus* (Lyric Hammersmith); *Red Ellen* (Northern Stage); *Dorian* (Reading Rep); *Missing Julie* (Theatre Clywd).

Television includes: *Prisoner C33* (BBC/Pioneer Productions).

Film includes: *Nanjing, Harm.*

Multidisciplinary work includes: *Nineteen Ways of Looking* (Chinese Arts Now); *At Home with the World* (Bagri Foundation); *Culture Mile* (London Symphony Orchestra).

British-Malaysian Artist and Composer Jasmin brings together the contemporary classical, electronics and sound art worlds to create powerful soundscapes and musical identities. A collaborator across various art forms including dance, word, film and VR, her music often explores otherness, memory and plays with a sense of narrative.

Her music and live productions have been performed across the UK and internationally with partners such as London Fashion Week, World Music Festival Shanghai, Edinburgh International Festival, Wilderness Festival, the Roundhouse, Shoreditch Town Hall, Barbican, Oxford Playhouse and the Royal Albert Hall. Her film scores have featured at festivals such as Sundance, SXSW, Toronto International Film Festival and the London Short Film Festival.

## Adi Gortler

### Movement Director

Previously at Jermyn Street Theatre: *The Anarchist*.

Theatre (as Movement Director) includes: *The Snow Queen* (Polka Theatre); *Baghdaddy, Jews. In Their Own Words* (Royal Court Theatre); *Antisemitism A (((Musical)))* (Camden People's Theatre); *Attempts On Her Life* (Guildhall); *How To Hold Your Breath, The Antipodes, Light Falls, Woyzeck, Pomona* (LAMDA); *Borders* ألسياج (Vault Festival/Drayton Arms/OSO Arts Centre).

Theatre (as Intimacy Director) includes: *The Shape Of Things* (Park Theatre); *How To Hold Your Breath* (LAMDA).

Theatre (as Director) includes: *I See in Colour* (International Children's Theatre Festival, Haifa); *As a Matter of Fact – The Post Truth Cabaret* (Habima Theatre/The Arab-Hebrew Theatre, Tzavta/ Haifa Theatre).

Adi Gortler (she/her) is a movement director, teacher, and theatremaker. She graduated with her MFA in Movement Directing and Teaching from the Royal Central School of Speech and Drama, and a B.Ed in Theatre Directing and Teaching from Seminar Ha'Kibbutzim College. At the heart of her practice lies a deep celebration of people and their individuality, leading to an environment where uniqueness and identities are cherished and expressed in the work of telling a story.

# Jamie Kubisch-Wiles

## Stage Manager

Theatre as Stage Manager includes: *1000 Ways The World Will End* (King's Head Theatre); *A Christmas Carol* 2021 and 2022; *A Midsummer Night's Dream* (Reading Rep Theatre); *Actors and Musical Theatre Showcases* (READ College).

Theatre as Assistant Stage Manager includes: *Potted Panto*, *DORIAN* (Reading Rep Theatre); *The Hound of the Baskervilles*, *One Million Tiny Plays About Britain*, *Prince and the Pauper* (The Watermill Theatre).

Jamie Kubisch-Wiles is a Reading-based freelance stage manager who completed the Andrew Lloyd Webber Traineeship for Assistant Stage and Production Management at The Watermill Theatre 2019.

# Woven Voices

Woven Voices is a London-based award-winning production company. It seeks to weave together different voices, native and migrant, in order to champion cross-cultural work. Stage projects include *Subject Mater* (Edinburgh Festival Fringe, Fringe First Award), *Bruises* (Tabard Theatre) and *Tartuffe* (Theatre Royal Haymarket). The company also produces short films and records their podcast series *Migreatives*, which features interviews with migrant creatives working in the UK.

## Acknowledgements

Thank you to Baba, Mum and Adrian.

Those without whom this play would not exist: Esme Alman, Eliza Bacon, Isabelle Clarke, Nick Collin, Sarah Davey-Hull, Bilal Hasna, Ella Hickson, Georgia Green, Stella Green, Will Maclean, Christian Ogunbanjo, Kwame Owusu, Harry Redding, Darren Sinnott, Talia Tobias, Nikhil Vyas, Ciaran Walsh.

All those who gave feedback, advice, spoke to me about the play, its themes, and their homes.

# The EU Killed My Dad

The problem was that we did not know whom we meant when we said 'we'.

*– Adrienne Rich, 'Notes Toward a Politics of Location'*

**Characters** (in order of appearance)

**Alien Lizard**
**Berker**
**Investigator One**
**Investigator Two**
**Elif**
**Doctor**
**Mustafa**
**Communist Revolutionary**
**Islamist Revolutionary**
**British Spy**
**American Corporal**
**Turkish Judge**
**Fellow Prisoner**
**Bahriye**
**Border Guard**
**Janice**
**Umut**

### Notes on casting

*This play was written for five actors.*

**Berker** *and* **Elif** *should only play themselves.*

### Notes on language

*UNDERLINED lines are not assigned because they should exist as separate from the rest of the dialogue. They are probably projections, but you can have your fun with them if you like.*

*When characters speak Turkish, we hear them in English. To everyone in the world of the play it is Turkish.*

*A dash – is used to indicate a particularly pointed interruption.*

*An ellipsis . . . marks a trailing off, a breather or a transition.*

*A Japanese maple tree in autumn. An* **Alien Lizard**. **Berker**.

*The* **Alien Lizard** *raises a gun and aims it at* **Berker**.

*Blackout.*

**2023**

*The garden.*

**Berker** *is in gardening clothes.*

**Investigator One** *asking the questions,* **Investigator Two** *floats, performatively absent-minded.*

**Berker**   Memory?

**Investigator One**   Memory is a good word.

**Berker**   It's not quite right . . . maybe . . . napkin?

**Investigator One**   Napkin? Napkin can't be right.

**Berker**   No . . .

**Investigator One**   Coincidence? Did you mean to say coincidence?

**Berker**   Oh . . . yeah that's kind of what I was trying to –

**Investigator One**   So – coincidence?

**Berker**   Are you writing that down?

**Investigator One**   Yeah?

**Berker**   No but it's not . . . not quite the right . . . no. In English we say 'serendipity'?

**Investigator One**   Seren-what?

**Berker**   'Serendipity'. Is there a Turkish word for that?

**Investigator One**   My English consists of: 'hello-goodbye-Coca-Cola-yespleaseonthetable'.

**Berker**   My Turkish is mostly from TV. Detective shows. Do you guys watch those or is it like taking the work home?

**Investigator One**   *Behzat?*

**Berker**   Of course.

**Investigator One**   The last one with the brother –

**Berker**   But then it was the dad and the sister who –

**Investigator One**   And that guy with the moustache.

**Berker**   Is it really like that in real life?

**Investigator One**   It can get pretty crazy . . .

**Berker**   Wow . . . so like have you –

**Investigator Two**   Let's just put down coincidence.

**Investigator Two** *gives* **Investigator One** *a look. He understands and hardens.*

**Berker**   Coincidence isn't quite right.

**Investigator Two**   It will do.

**Berker**   But it's not quite . . . it's not quite what happened. If you want to know what happened: 'serendipity'.

**Investigator Two**   We'll make a note of it.

**Berker**   Thank you.

**Investigator One**   Can you spell that for me?

**Investigator Two**   You've got a nice house, Mr Walker –

**Berker**   Just Berker is fine. Watch the roses please. Freshly planted.

**Investigator Two**   I like this part of the country. I used to come near here to visit my grandma, help her with the olive harvest. Must be a big change from London for you. Hot summers you guys get here. Yeah. It's all just plastic landfill now, isn't it? Recycling they call it and then burn it. Not the same. But you've got something here. Nice garden, you take care of things. We appreciate that. It's the kind of thing that makes a good police officer. Attention to detail, you see. That's what this job is. My colleague and I we've been paying attention to some details, and we want to ask for your help to clear them up for us. There was a murder here a few years ago, as I'm sure you remember, but a perpetrator was never identified. '15 July' the file says. As though a date can be held responsible for a murder. Now you don't think a date can be held responsible for a murder, do you? So we're here to see if we can find some better answers. The kind that satisfies men like you and me. You understand. Attention to detail. Now how does that sound? We'll ask you some questions and you just answer honestly. With that famous attention.

**Berker**    I already gave my statement. Years ago. What made you –

**Investigator One**    It's a – oh. In English they say 'Cold Case'. Like the TV show? Also a good one if you haven't seen it

**Berker**    You're re-opening the case?

**Investigator One**    Instructions from above. All culprits of 15 July must be brought to justice.

**Investigator Two**    To move on we must first understand what made us move in the first place, you see. To write the future we must complete the story of the past.

**Berker**    Should I be calling a lawyer or –

**Investigator Two**    Sure you can do that. It's your right. Of course, if you do call a lawyer we'll have to make this all official, take you down to the station. You might spend a night or two there depending on the boss's mood.

**Investigator One**    Or we just do it here. In your lovely garden. Have a little chat. You practise your Turkish. You'd save us a hell of a lot of paperwork.

**Berker**    I thought this was just a formality.

**Investigator Two**    Mr Walker, between us, your co-operation would really mean a lot. I was meant to retire nine months ago and they tasked me with 15 July. You understand? They need answers before the election. It's part of the . . . narrative. Your father. This. He's the last one. All

I've got to do is point the finger. Then I'm done. My legacy. You understand.

**Berker** What if I don't want to talk about it?

**Investigator Two** Well, that would be awfully . . . what's the word I'm looking for here in English . . .

**Investigator One** 'Suspicious'?

**Investigator Two** Such a strange language.

**Investigator One** If someone is 'suspicious'. Of course, then we must treat him differently. 'Suspiciously'.

**Investigator Two** You wouldn't want us to point our fingers in an inconvenient direction now would you?

**Berker** What do you want to know?

**Investigator Two** Let's start with the beginning. 'Serendipity'. When did you first learn about your father's death?

**Berker** 16 July 2016. Day I met Elif. Hard to forget. I got here, to this house. It was the address I had for him, but no one was around. The neighbour pointed me to the hospital where I found Elif.

**Investigator Two** Identifying the body. What was she like?

**Berker** She was . . . she was just Elif. Nothing can touch her, always the calmest person in the room. Hard to the bone. Empathy isn't really part of her . . . vocabulary. Didn't really leave much space for processing.

**2016**

*A hospital.*

**Berker** This isn't how I, erm, expected. Us meeting. I sort of imagined something different? I'm Berker, your brother.

**Elif** Elif. What are you doing in Küçükköy?

**Berker**    I – God is he actually . . .

**Elif**    You should have gotten a message. I messaged his contact list this morning.

**Berker**    When did he . . .?

**Elif**    Yesterday. This was all in the text.

**Berker**    A potato.

**Elif**    What?

**Berker**    That's what I did yesterday. I sat on the sofa watching this alien documentary and I ate a potato. Baked.

*A* **Doctor** *arrives.*

**Doctor**    Apologies for the wait. We're obviously very busy after yesterday. My condolences.

**Elif**    Have you got a cause yet?

**Berker**    What's she saying?

**Elif**    One second.

**Doctor**    Hello, English little little. Mix English-Turkish, yes?

**Elif**    You can just tell me in Turkish.

**Berker**    Mix. Yeah great.

**Doctor**    Mustafa, ah how do you say it in English –

**Elif**    Just tell me and I'll translate.

**Doctor**    He was shot. There wasn't much doubt of course but the official cause of death now is the gunshot wound.

**Elif**    Are you sure?

**Berker**    What did she say?

**Doctor**    What do you mean am I sure? He was shot by a gun.

**Elif**    Couldn't it have been something else?

**Doctor**    I'm sorry, miss, but – no. It couldn't.

**Berker**   What is she saying?

**Doctor**   Mr Mustafa . . . ah . . . word . . . pew pew.

*The* **Doctor** *mimes shooting a gun.*

**Berker**   Pew pew?

**Doctor**   Pew pew. Dead.

**Berker**   Oh my God.

**Doctor**   Yes of course.

**Berker**   Thank you.

**Doctor**   Yes of course.

*The* **Doctor** *hands them both a lollipop.*

**Berker**   A lollipop?

**Doctor**   Yes of course.

*The* **Doctor** *leaves.*


**2023**

**Investigator Two**   You find out your dad was shot – what are you thinking?

**Berker**   Everything was so sudden. It was hard to process any of it in the moment.

**Investigator One**   You just went along with things.

**Berker**   I –

**Investigator One**   You just accepted whatever you were told. I thought you were into your investigative shows?

**Berker**   I am.

**Investigator One**   You seem rather naive, Mr Berker.

**Berker**   I did a good job. You seem so confident why haven't you figured out what happened?

**Investigator One**   251 people died that night. We've been assigned to seventeen of those and of course we arrested perpetrators for sixteen of those cases already. I am in line for station chief and that man right there is about to retire as one of the finest officers this country has ever seen. Show some damn respect.

**Berker**   Yeah, I don't doubt you arrested people. Whether you found those responsible is a different question . . .

**Investigator One**   What the hell are you trying to imply?

**Investigator Two**   Let's just get back to the events of the day. Ease up. We're expected to have answers by tonight.

**Berker**   Don't mischaracterise what I did. I did something.

**Investigator Two**   What happens next, Mr Walker?

**Berker**   We came here. She had to sort through his things. Wasn't much for talking. Until you wanted her to be quiet and then she couldn't shut up.


## 2016

**Elif** *comes in and out of the scene carrying boxes.* **Berker** *watches her.*

**Berker**   You really look like him. Last time I saw him he must have been about the age I am now. But you look more like him.

*Beat.*

**Berker**   My sister.

**Elif**   Half-sister.

**Berker**   It's good to meet you. Finally.

**Elif**   Uh-huh.

**Berker**   What you doing?

**Elif**   Collecting things. We need to sort out the house and then the garden. Lots to do.

**Berker**   Your English is really good.

*Beat.*

You like to garden?

**Elif**   Uh-huh.

**Berker**   It's not really my area of expertise . . . all the dirt and . . . I'm more a hot chocolate and TV kind of person.

**Elif**   Uh-huh.

**Berker**   Do you not want to . . . I mean we should be, you know. Siblings. Our father has . . . we should. Mark the moment. Talk about memories and things.

**Elif**   I don't have time to mark the moment. Death is admin.

**Berker**   That can wait. For now let's commemorate –

**Elif**   I don't know you.

**Berker**   So let's get to know –

**Elif**   The funeral is tonight and by then the house needs to be sorted out because the buyers are arriving this afternoon. So I need to sort out a house and then I need to get ready for a funeral.

**Berker**   Let me help then.

**Elif**   No thank you. I have no issue with you. Really. You seem nice. Maybe one day we can sit down and do the whole 'oh wow we have the same eyebrows isn't that crazy' thing, but I don't have time. Okay?

**Berker**   Can you at least tell me what happened to him. I mean pew pew. He was shot?

**Elif**   I don't know.

**Berker**    What do you mean?

**Elif**    I don't know.

**Berker**    You don't know what happened to him?

**Elif**    No.

**Berker**    What have the police said?

**Elif**    Police is pointless.

**Berker**    Usually in a murder case the police investigate –

**Elif**    Who says murder?

**Berker**    So it was sui–

**Elif**    I don't know.

**Berker**    So let's see what the police –

**Elif**    No police.

**Berker**    Fine. Then let's find our own answers.

**Elif** (*laughing*)    Okay.

**Berker**    I'm serious.

**Elif**    You want to play pretend policeman? Alien documentary man?

**Berker**    I'm a police officer.

**Elif**    What?

**Berker**    That made you pay attention. Yeah. Detective Walker. Nice to meet you.

**Elif**    He never said.

**Berker**    So he talked about me?

**Elif**    What are you doing here?

**Berker**    To see my –

**Elif**    After fifteen years you suddenly decide to see him? No reason?

**Berker**    I thought I was finally . . . you know.

**Elif**    I don't.

**Berker**    Coming home.

**Elif**    You don't live here.

**Berker**    But I could.

**Elif**    You live in London. Why would you want to come here?

**Berker**    London's . . . loud.

**Elif**    You only just noticed?

**Berker**    I feel like I belong here. Even this house, these walls, I mean you can feel history in these walls. Family. Strong foundations. I think I could make a life here.

**Elif**    I told you. I'm selling the house.

**Berker**    That's a bit quick don't you think?

**Elif**    Why wait?

**Berker**    Why wait more than a day after your father died to sell your family home? I don't know, man, maybe to have some fudging respect?

**Elif**    Fudging?

**Berker**    It's like a replacement for the other – for –

**Elif**    Fucking.

**Berker**    Oh. Yeah. Fucking. Wasn't sure if that was disrespectful or.

**Elif**    You think I don't say fucking?

**Berker**    I wasn't sure –

**Elif**    Because I'm Turkish or because I'm a woman? Or both?

**Berker**    Do you really think this is what he would have wanted?

**Elif**    It's time to leave. It's been time for a while.

**Berker**    It's not yours to sell.

**Elif**    I'm his daughter.

**Berker**    Is there a will?

*Beat.*

So I have as much right to it as you.

**Elif**    You've never even lived here.

**Berker**    I'm his son.

**Elif**    That's why you're here.

**Berker**    Don't be daft.

**Elif**    You British can smell an opportunity for money from a mile –

**Berker**    I'm not British. I'm Turkish.

**Elif**    Whatever you are, I don't trust you. Why are you here?

**Berker**    I'm not trying to take the house.

**Elif**    For someone who isn't interested in the house you sure talk about the house a lot.

**Berker**    I just wanted to see my dad.

**Elif**    Baba.

**Berker**    What?

**Elif**    Call him baba.

*Beat.*

**Berker**    I don't care about the house. I want to know what happened to him.

**Elif**   There are a million different reasons why someone dies. You can't just isolate a single incident and –

**Berker**   Okay so if I shot you in the head with a gun am I not the cause of your death?

**Elif**   Are you? What about the gun? Or the . . . the social conditions that made you do it?

**Berker**   The social condition is you're annoying.

**Elif**   You're annoying.

**Berker**   Someone or something is to blame. And I, we, need to know.

**Elif**   It's not that simple.

**Berker**   We need to be able to point the finger and say: you!

**Elif**   What if we don't like what we find?

**Berker**   At least we'll know. Will you help me?

**Elif**   I told you I'm busy –

**Berker**   I – I need you.

**Elif**   Why?

**Berker**   You're my sister.

*Beat.*

You do this for me you can have the house. It's all yours, the whole inheritance and you can do with it what you want.

**Elif**   Half-sister.

**Berker**   So?

**Elif**   I get the house?

**Berker**   Scout's honour.

**Berker**   Do you have any leads?

**Elif**   Why do you care so much? You didn't even know him.

**Berker**    We need to start with the evidence.

**Elif**    Why would you give me the house just because I'm playing your game?

**Berker**    Do you want the house or do you want to talk about our feelings? Your choice.

**Elif**    You have until the funeral tonight. No exceptions. Where do we start?

**Berker**    Always start with those closest to the suspect.

*A pin board full of newspaper clippings and images, connected by string appears.*

**Berker**    What's going on here?

**Elif**    Baba and his obsessions.

**Berker** *finds a picture of an alien lizard connected with string to a picture of Hillary Clinton.*

**Berker**    And this is . . .?

**Elif**    Alien lizard?

**Berker**    Right. Alien lizard . . .

**Elif**    Can you not touch it please. Isn't it evidence?

**Berker**    True . . . so! Our first suspect.

# Option One: Elif's Mother

**Berker** *hangs up a picture of* **Elif**'s *mother onto the pin board.*

**Berker**   Always start with love.

**Elif**   What do you know about love?

**Berker**   Hey! I've loved.

**Elif**   Baked potato doesn't count.

**Berker**   As if you're any better.

**Elif**   I have someone.

**Berker**   Bullshit.

**Elif**   I do. We're in love.

**Berker**   Sure you are.

**Elif**   His name is Umut.

**Berker**   Uh-huh.

**Elif**   He's like really hot.

**Berker**   You don't have to lie to impress me.

**Elif**   Meeting Umut was the first time in my life that I understood what life is meant to be about. He's the love of my life. So make fun of it all you want and enjoy your potatoes.

*Beat.*

**Berker**   So. Your mum.


**2023**

**Investigator One**   What made you think of her mother?

**Berker**   A shared past.

**Investigator One**   She had a motive?

**Berker**   How much do you know about Mustafa's return to Turkey?

**1980**

**Mustafa** *enters. The* **Communist Revolutionary** *enters. They shake hands.*

**Communist**   Welcome home, comrade.

**Mustafa**   Uh-huh.

**Elif**   Our baba returns to Turkey ready to fight a revolution.

**Berker**   That's one version.

**Elif**   His country has just suffered another military coup and he is ready to –

**Berker**   He returns to Turkey after he abandons his family in London –

**Elif**   He returns to fight for our freedom, our future –

**Berker**   He returns because he couldn't get a visa in Britain.

**Elif**   He comes home determined.

**Berker**   He comes back . . . confused.

**Communist**   We need more men like you. Brave men returning to protect their country. I can't stand watching those cowards in their kebab restaurants in Berlin and Vienna and London.

**Mustafa**   Yes.

**Communist**   Although revolution is of course international.

**Mustafa**   Uh-huh.

**Communist**   But first here.

**Mustafa**   Yes.

**Communist**   You see as soon as you walked through that door and shook my hand you became one of us: a revolutionary.

**Mustafa**   Uh-huh.

**Communist**   And that means pure freedom, the freest freedom you can imagine.

**Mustafa**   Yes.

**Communist**   Of course that's why you're here. But freedom is never safe.

**Mustafa**   No.

**Communist**   The Americans, the British, the Islamists, they are all enemies of revolution. Enemies of freedom.

**Mustafa**   Yes.

**Communist**   We have a mission for you. It could be deadly. But it's for DEMOCRACY. So. What do you think?

**Mustafa**   What's the mission?

**Communist**   You're our man on the inside.

*The* **Communist Revolutionary** *turns into a* **British Spy**.

**Spy**   Your name, chap.

**Mustafa**   Mustafa.

**Spy**   Turkish.

**Mustafa**   Yes.

**Spy**   First rate. Our man on the inside.

**Mustafa**   Inside what?

**Spy**   Inside all of it. In them, in us. In between. We're spies.

**Mustafa**   I am?

**Spy**   Sure you are.

**Mustafa**   Uh-huh.

**Spy**   Now do you love your country, old chap?

**Mustafa**   My . . .

**Spy**   Does your heart beat and bleed the values of the free world? Are you on the right side of history?

**Mustafa**   Which side are you on?

**Spy**   I know just the job for you.

*The* **British Spy** *turns into an* **Islamist Revolutionary**.

**Islamist**   Do you love your God, brother?

**Mustafa**   Yes.

**Islamist**   Do you find yourself up late at night questioning whether your life is lived truly and purely in the service of Allah?

**Mustafa**   Uh-huh.

**Islamist**   Brother, the forces of imperialism have corrupted our people. Even me, even you. Our people hate themselves. We live in a Muslim country run by people who hate Islam. We live in a country run by men educated in Paris, Oxford, New York. Leaders that would rather be French than Turkish.

**Mustafa**   Right.

**Islamist**   Must we not awaken our people's consciousness? Must we not end this self-hatred? Must we not say no to greedy uncle America? Must we not ensure, as it is written, 'that no one other than God can limit human freedom'?

**Mustafa**   Yes.

**Islamist**   I want you to meet someone.

*The* **Islamist Revolutionary** *turns into an* **American Sergeant**.

**Sergeant**   You're our man on the inside, Mustafa.

**Mustafa**    Uh-huh.

**Sergeant**    We've got those commies surrounded thanks to you. How did you come to love DEMOCRACY so much?

**Mustafa**    Erm . . .

**Sergeant**    You grew up here didn't you? In this beautiful exotic godforsaken but sensual hot and cold tactically well-positioned geographically convenient not a satellite state not a colony but definitely our colony country?

**Mustafa**    Yes.

**Sergeant**    But your English is miraculous.

**Mustafa**    I lived in London.

**Sergeant**    London – a city of culture! Why did you come back? To protect your country from the commies?

**Mustafa**    Uh-huh.

**Sergeant**    You're not luring us into a trap are you, boy?

**Mustafa**    No.

*The **American Sergeant** turns into a **Turkish Judge**.*

**Judge**    How dare you have lured our American friends into a trap?

**Mustafa**    For democracy.

**Judge**    Who do you belong to?

**Mustafa**    I don't know.

**Judge**    Who did you not betray?

**Mustafa**    Democracy.

**Judge**    Pfff. Are you a Turk? A communist? Brit? What and why!

**Mustafa**    I don't know.

**Judge**   Do you not see that our American friends are liberating us? That they are the ones giving us democracy?

**Mustafa**   No.

**Judge**   That without their help and their glorious weapons and glorious Coca-Cola and glorious Ford Mustangs and glorious Marlboro Red we would be nothing? We would be further away from Europe than ever. And don't you want to be European? Don't you want our wish of glorious European democracy to finally come true? Perhaps one day we will live in a country that speaks a glorious German and a glorious French or even, dare I say it, English, and we will read Shakespeare and Goethe and we will sing John Lennon, and we will be glorious, and we will be a democracy. Do you not want that?

**Mustafa**   No.

**Judge**   Five years' hard labour. Next!

*The* **Judge** *turns into a* **Fellow Prisoner**. *They work their hard labour.*

**Fellow Prisoner**   What you in for friend?

**Mustafa**   Democracy.

**Fellow Prisoner**   Hah! Same. Friend. Same.

*They keep working.*

**Fellow Prisoner**   I shot my dad for democracy. See, friend, we're farmers from down near Izmir and we had this acre of land that was unused. See my dad, he's a religious man and he said this is the good acre. This is the acre for Allah. This acre stays untouched, pure, it is to make space. We were poor, our farm was small, and all the food we grew we had to sell, so there was never much left for us. One freezing winter I turn to my father and I say: Dear father, my sister is starving, my brothers are thirsty, and I am so short, why don't we grow some potatoes on the acre so we can eat? And he says no, this acre belongs to Allah. And that year on 1

January one of my brothers died. And the next year again, I ask my father, my teeth chattering from the cold, father please, why don't we grow some carrots on the acre. It is so beautiful, they will grow so quickly. Don't let another son die. And my father slaps me across the face and says: Don't you fear your God? On 1 January my other brother died. Finally, the next year, I go to my sister and I say sister, we cannot live any longer in this hunger, no human should live like this, our father has betrayed us for his fear of Allah, is a selfish fear and she slapped me across the face and said brother, respect your father. So, friend. What would you do in this situation? Would you spend another year starving, narrowly escaping death or would you take action, friend? For democracy, friend. So one freezing night, as the house lay asleep, I pick up the rifle and I say to my father: rise, father, rise and he looks at me and he says, don't you fear anything? And in the back my sister she is crying and pleading saying brother please, please don't do this, but I have made up my mind, the acre must be soiled, there must be food, purity does not fill an empty stomach, does not keep you warm against the bitter cold so I take my father to the empty acre, and it is dark, except the moonlight and I point the gun, the gun I have seen my father use so many times before and I point it at him and I pull the trigger. And again. See, friend, what I didn't expect was that there wasn't just blood, but also all the insides and the brain and the guts went flying everywhere. And the soil was soiled and that very night in the freezing cold I dug a grave for my father and laid a potato in the grave with him and the next spring, a potato grew out the ground.

*Beat.*

And what about you? What did you do for democracy?

**Bahriye**, **Elif**'s *mum, enters.*

**Bahriye**   I can help you.

**Mustafa**   That's what they all say.

**Bahriye**  You have a case.

**Mustafa**  A case of what?

**Berker**  Oh! This is your mum?

**Elif**  Shhh.

**Bahriye**  Human rights abuses, wrongful imprisonment, I could even bring in the British, you have . . . people in London?

**Mustafa**  No. No, not London.

**Bahriye**  They could help.

**Mustafa**  I want nothing to do with Britain

**Bahriye**  Your case it's . . . hard.

**Mustafa**  I've heard that before.

**Bahriye**  I could help you . . . release.

**Mustafa**  Boy, do I need that.

**Bahriye**  Empty it all out.

**Mustafa**  What would you like in return?

**Bahriye**  Push the right buttons.

**Mustafa**  I think I can find those.

**Bahriye**  I could bring this to the Europeans.

**Mustafa**  Wait I'm confused

**Bahriye**  They could help. They have a lot of sway over the regime.

**Mustafa**  What are we talking about?

**Bahriye**  I have a connect at the European Court of Justice. She could join us.

**Mustafa**  Oh – the three of us?

**Bahriye**  She'd have a whole team behind her.

**Mustafa**   That sounds overwhelming.

**Bahriye**   I'd be overseeing.

**Mustafa**   But the Europeans . . .

**Bahriye**   They might go soft just when we need them.

**Mustafa**   And at what cost?

**Bahriye**   We have to do something.

**Mustafa**   What about just you and me?

**Bahriye**   Me and you.

**Mustafa**   Here?

**Bahriye**   No one's watching.

**Mustafa** *and* **Bahriye** *kiss.*

**Elif**   Ew. Stop! Don't need this.

**Berker**   Details matter.

**Elif**   She helped him avoid torture and I guess he helped her avoid loneliness. I was born soon after he was released. They were moving forward, a new life, a new beginning. The past was in the past. They moved us to the countryside, Küçükköy, a place where politics didn't reach. Where they felt safe from the violence and tumultuousness of the city. Baba became a gardener and my mother opened a free legal clinic, the first and only in a 100-mile radius.

**Mustafa**   I counted fifty buds on the daffodil I planted last year. None are open yet, but if this warm weather continues they should be out within the week.

**Bahriye**   I saved three innocent men from torture while breastfeeding our daughter.

**Berker**   And they lived happily ever after?

**2016**

*We are back in the garden.* **Mustafa** *exits.* **Bahriye** *ages.*

**Bahriye**    No.

**Elif**    Mum! How long have you been standing there?

**Bahriye**    Long enough.

**Berker**    What are you saying? Is this your mum?

**Bahriye**    Who's this?

**Berker**    Sorry, I don't speak Turkish!

**Elif**    This is Berker. My, you know.

**Berker**    HELLO. NICE. TO. MEET. YOU.

**Elif**    Berker.

**Berker**    I AM YOUR HUSBAND'S FIRST SON. FIRST. SON. CHILD. ME. NUMBER ONE.

**Elif**    Berker.

**Bahriye**    Why is he shouting?

**Elif**    Berker, calm down.

**Berker**    SORRY.

**Bahriye**    English. No good. *Parles-tu français?*

**Berker**    No . . . erm. *Pardon.*

**Bahriye**    *Español?*

**Berker**    ENGLISH.

**Bahriye**    Okay. English. Okay.

**Berker**    THANK YOU FOR COMING. WE WANT TO ASK SOME QUESTIONS ABOUT MUSTAFA'S DEATH.

**Bahriye**    Too many.

**Elif**    Maybe I should just translate.

**Berker**   OH YEAH GOOD – Sorry. Good idea.

**Bahriye**   I was surprised to hear from you, Elif.

**Elif**   I – can we not do that right now.

**Bahriye**   I'm only saying I was –

**Elif**   He wants to know more about Baba.

**Berker**   Yes. Baba.

**Bahriye**   Why are you coming to me to talk about your father? I haven't seen that man in years.

**Elif**   She says she is very upset about it all.

**Berker**   Ask where she was yesterday. (*Looks up on his phone.*) Dün?

**Bahriye**   Yesterday? I was at home glued to the TV like everyone else.

**Elif**   She says she was at home.

**Bahriye**   Where were you?

**Elif**   Me?

**Bahriye**   Weren't you working?

**Elif**   Well, yeah but –

**Bahriye**   Were you involved in any –

**Elif**   No! How could you –

**Bahriye**   What about Umut?

**Berker**   What's going on?

**Elif**   I don't want to talk about Umut.

**Bahriye**   Well, was he working?

**Elif**   We're trying to ask you about Baba.

**Bahriye**   Your baba died last night, you don't think your little coup had something to do with it?

**Elif**   No one was meant to die.

**Bahriye**   So you were involved.

**Elif**   I didn't do anything.

**Bahriye**   You drag me to this parochial shithole to say goodbye to your idiot of a father and you have the audacity to interrogate me with your own guilt?

**Elif**   I didn't do anything.

**Bahriye**   Was Umut working?

**Elif**   We're asking about you.

**Bahriye**   Well, I don't work for the military.

**Berker**   Military? She works for the military? *Asker.*

**Elif**   Are you seriously using your phone right now?

**Bahriye**   *Asker.* Yes. *Asker.*

**Berker**   You?

**Bahriye** (*shakes her head*)   Umut.

**Berker**   Umut?

**Bahriye**   Umut. (*Points at* **Elif**.)

**Berker**   Wait – your hot boyfriend Umut?

**Bahriye**   Yes.

**Berker**   Your hot boyfriend works for the military?

**Elif** *shrugs*.

**Berker**   Why didn't you say?

**Elif**   Why should I say?

**Berker**   What are you hiding from me?

**Elif**   Nothing! You've just interrogated my poor mother because you have some weird obsession with pointing fingers at random people –

**Berker**    We have to go through every option.

*He translates on his phone.*

Who dies father?

**Bahriye**    What?

**Berker**    Who dies my father?

**Bahriye**    I don't know.

**Berker**    Who hates?

**Bahriye**    Your mother.

**Berker**    What?

**Elif**    You heard her.

**Bahriye**    Mother. You.

**Berker**    Why?

**Elif**    Well, well, well.

**Berker**    I don't understand.

**Bahriye**    History.

**Berker**    What does that mean? Elif, translate please.

**Bahriye** *takes* **Berker**'s *phone and looks something up.*

**Bahriye**    His-tory. His-tory.

**Berker**    Because of history? My mum hates my father because of history?

**Bahriye**    Story. Yes.

**Berker**    I don't understand.

**Bahriye**    I need to get ready for the funeral. I will see you later.

**Elif**    Bye, Mum.

**Bahriye**    We still need to talk.

**Berker**    What do you mean? Don't go. His story? What does that mean? Don't –

**Bahriye** *leaves.*

**Elif**    We both know what that means.

**Berker**    No?

**Elif**    We've been approaching this whole investigation all wrong.

**Berker**    What are you talking about?

**Elif**    Why would someone travel to see his estranged father for no reason, and why would that fall on the exact day after his father died.

**Berker**    I was eating a potato!

**Elif**    I thought you were here for the money.

**Berker**    I'm not.

**Elif**    But you're here to cover your tracks.

## _Option Two: Berker's Mum_

**Elif** _hangs up a picture of_ **Berker**_'s mum._

**Berker**   You can't be serious.

**Elif**   History.

**Berker**   My mum won't even use mousetraps, how is she meant to have killed a person?

**Elif**   Sounds like you're deflecting.

**Berker**   So my mother who's never hurt a thing in her life flies out and somehow finds a gun and then shoots him and disappears before anyone notices her even being in the country?

**Elif**   She had motive didn't she?

**Berker**   Because of things that happened thirty years ago?

**Elif**   If there's one thing you learn living in this country is that letting go of the past is not something humans are generally good at doing.

**Berker**   This is ludicrous. You're wasting our time. Once the funeral starts it's too late to –

**Elif**   If you've got nothing to hide, you've got nothing to fear.


**2023**

**Investigator Two**   History? What does she mean by that?

**Berker**   We both, erm, we both understood her to mean the past. His story.

**Investigator Two**   So your mother had motive to kill him?

**Berker**   No! This was one of Elif's mental theories. A way to deflect from what's really going on.

**Investigator One**    It sounds like you're deflecting here, pal.

**Berker**    No, I –

**Investigator Two**    Why don't you start from the beginning. The whole story.

**Berker**    Which version do you want – hers or mine?


**1971**

**Mustafa** *enters. During this entire section he acts out the children's narration.*

**Elif**    1971. Baba arrives in the UK aged nineteen. He's got no money, no possessions, apart from a tiny slip of paper that says:

**Mustafa**    Thompsen Road, Haringey,

**Elif**    And a small blue briefcase that he –

*A blue briefcase appears.*

**Berker**    Red.

**Elif**    What?

**Berker**    Red briefcase.

*A red briefcase appears.*

**Elif**    Blue.

**Berker**    I've seen it, it's red.

**Elif**    It's blue, I literally still –

**Berker**    It's red. Can we just agree and move on?

**Elif**    It's blue. You want to be an investigator you need details.

**Berker**    Why don't we just say it's purple? Sound fair?

**Elif**    Fine.

*A purple briefcase appears.*

**Berker**   A small *purple* briefcase that he inherited from his dad.

**Elif**   Who's also a prick, but that's a different story.

**Mustafa** *picks up the purple briefcase.*

**Elif**   He arrives in the UK after his country has just been fucked by a military takeover

**Berker**   Yeah, yeah.

**Elif**   Funded by the Americans.

**Berker**   Whatever.

**Elif**   I mean you don't leave unless you've got nothing to lose or something to prove.

**Berker**   And he kinda had both. So he gets to the border and –

*A* **Border Guard** *appears.*

**Border Guard**   Welcome to the UK.

**Mustafa**   Thank you.

**Border Guard**   Visa?

**Mustafa**   Mustafa.

**Border Guard**   Do you have a visa?

**Mustafa**   Thank you.

**Border Guard**   Visa? Entry permit. Do. You. Have. One?

**Mustafa**   Mustafa.

**Border Guard**   Mate what the hell are you saying?

**Mustafa**   Mustafa. Me. Mustafa.

**Border Guard**   Visa? Do you have a visa? You need permission to enter a country, you bloody –

**Berker**  It's the seventies.

**Elif**  Sure, things were a bit different.

**Berker**  Somehow he manages to get through, they give him a tourist visa or something and he arrives in

**Mustafa**  Thompsen Road, Haringey.

**Elif**  Where he lives with, like, fifteen other people

**Berker**  And spends all his free time watching *Hawaii Five-O* to improve his English.

**Mustafa** *hums the* Hawaii Five-O *theme tune.*

**Berker**  Detective shows have always been his favourite.

**Elif**  Meanwhile, he finds work in a kebab shop aptly named:

**Mustafa**  Kebab House.

**Elif**  Which conveniently leaves its employee paperwork untouched in a box in the back.

*A box of paperwork appears.*

**Berker**  Including their visa status.

**Elif**  It's generous. They give people a chance.

**Berker**  It's reckless.

**Elif**  It's in the Kebab House that Mustafa meets your mum, Janice –

**Berker**  Who's on her way home from a night out.

**Berker**'s *mum* **Janice** *appears.*

**Mustafa**  What can I get you?

**Janice**  I'm vegetarian.

**Mustafa**  I won't tell anyone if you don't.

**Janice**  My name's Janice.

**Mustafa**    Mustafa.

**Elif**    She sits down and her eyes don't leave his. It takes her four hours to finish that kebab. They just sit and chat all night and by the end she goes back to his place and –

**Berker**    That's not what happened.

**Elif**    This is what happened. He told me.

**Berker**    It's not true. What really happened:

**Janice**    I'm vegetarian.

**Mustafa**    I won't tell if you don't.

**Janice**    Umm . . . I mean can you just not put meat in it?

**Mustafa**    Just bread with salad?

**Janice**    You could put cheese in it?

**Mustafa**    That's a nice idea. Cheese. 'Vegetarian kebab.'

**Berker**    And she gets her kebab and leaves. The next day Mustafa convinces his boss of the market niche that is vegetarian kebabs, so Kebab House becomes the first place in London to proudly serve a variety of vegetarian kebabs. Janice becomes a regular.

**Janice**    I like the new menu.

**Mustafa**    You inspired it.

**Janice**    Did I?

**Mustafa**    'You could just put cheese in it.'

**Janice**    And you did.

**Berker**    And then she starts eating meat again so they don't see each other for two years. She dates another guy and then a woman and then another guy and –

**Mustafa**    It's you!

**Janice**    Oh yeah.

**Mustafa**    Thought I'd never see you again.

**Janice**    Here I am.

**Berker**    And finally, two years after he first wanted to he –

**Mustafa**    Would you . . . like to . . . eat together sometime?

**Janice**    Are you asking me out?

**Mustafa**    It wouldn't be kebab. It would be nice.

**Janice**    I like kebab.

**Berker**    And that's when they start dating.

*Beat.*

**Elif**    Great.

**Berker**    Old Mr Sönmez always saw Dad as a son, so when he retires he hands over the shop to Mustafa, who renames it.

**Mustafa**    Kebab Home.

**Elif**    Fitting.

**Berker**    Again, Mr Sönmez doesn't bother with the paperwork.

*Another box of paperwork appears.*

**Elif**    It's complicated and his English isn't good so he just tells Baba that the shop is his.

**Berker**    Without doing the legal work that is required to hand over –

**Elif**    But everyone knew that Baba owned the shop.

**Berker**    Eventually they settle down into a small basement flat with a rear garden in Dalston.

**Elif**    This is where Baba picks up the gardening hobby that remains his passion for the rest of his life.

**Berker**   Mum never quite got the hang of either, but we did always have nice daffodils in spring.

**Elif**   They never get married, a romantic sort of gesture towards free-spirited love –

**Berker**   He's illegal.

**Elif**   That's a bleak way of putting it.

**Berker**   He doesn't have the papers. His three-month tourist visa ran out about nine years ago and he's been dreaming of two fellas with machine guns tearing down his door and throwing him in the Thames ever since.

**Elif**   No tact.

**Berker**   And then 1979 happens.

**Janice**   Oh dear, oh dear, oh dear, oh dear.

**Mustafa**   What's wrong?

**Janice**   She's won.

**Elif**   And that was obviously a problem.

**Berker**   For many reasons.

**Elif**   Not least because

*More and more paperwork appears. It is scattered all over the stage.* **Mustafa** *tries to make order out of the chaos of papers.*

**Janice** (*reading*)   'We believe in holding out the clear prospect of an end to immigration . . . We call for the immediate deportation of all illegal immigrants.'

**Mustafa**   That bloody b–

**Berker**   So now he's pissing himself.

**Elif**   And he's got a son who's pissing himself.

**Berker**   Cos he's a baby.

**Elif**   A pissy baby.

**Berker**  And he's got a wife.

**Janice**  Who hardly has a moment to piss.

**Berker**  And he doesn't have papers.

**Janice**  And he doesn't have the fucking papers.

**Berker**  When you hear about illegal immigrants you usually think about people sneaking through fences and hiding in dingy smuggler lairs. And maybe that's true. It's probably true. But this is also what it looks like.

**Janice**  Starting a family. Being in love. Having a child. Owning a restaurant. It might be some good immigrant bullshit, but it's also not hurting anyone.

**Elif**  So he leaves? This is when he leaves, right?

**Berker**  He spends the next year quite literally pissing himself. He's too afraid to go out, too afraid to stay in.

**Janice**  The month after Thatcher's election he spends every day on the phone to some lawyer or councillor, but it's all –

**Berker**  Please hold.

**Janice**  And he's been holding.

**Berker**  Please hold.

**Mustafa**  I am holding! I am Mr Holding.

**Janice**  And all of them say the same thing.

**Elif**  You don't have the right papers?

**Berker**  Every morning he joins the four-hour queue outside the Home Office.

**Mustafa** *joins the queue. After a moment he turns around.*

**Elif**  Why is he turning around?

**Berker**    Men in grey suits and stick-on smiles start coming to the restaurant, coming to old Mr Sönmez's house, asking for more papers and papers

**Janice**    But Mr Sönmez is old and tired and

**Berker**    Well, it turns out the boxes in the back should have been filled out years ago.

**Janice**    And Mustafa doesn't know what to do with them.

**Elif** *starts looking through the paperwork.*

**Elif**    Written with words so very different from the English language he thought he had mastered.

**Berker**    When finally, with all their money spent on lawyers and documents, they find papers that might be the right papers –

**Janice** *and* **Mustafa** *find the right papers.*

**Berker**    They're too scared.

**Janice**    Come on.

**Mustafa**    What if it's too much of a gamble? What if the application gives them a reason? What if it tells them who I am and then they kick me out? What if they arrest you? What if – I can't!

*He rips up the paperwork.*

**Berker**    He loses the restaurant.

**Janice**    I start working as a typist. We weren't rich before but now we are squeezed

**Berker**    He feels useless. Weak. Like he's disappointing everyone.

**Janice**    He spends his days wiling away at home.

**Berker**    His only comfort is the garden, which unlike him actually begins to take root.

**Janice**   Everything in that 10 x 3 square foot radius, from the crocuses to the daffodils, is living in harmony. Apart from Mustafa.

**Berker**   My only memory is the image of him holding a daffodil, not moving, just staring. Like he'd forgotten how to exist.

**Janice**   A year goes by and the mundanity is the worst. The waiting. The boredom.

**Elif**   But how does she feel about it?

**Janice**   I –

**Berker**   She's fine.

**Elif**   She doesn't seem fine. She seems like she has quite a bit of resentment towards a man who basically gave up on life.

**Berker**   Well not quite. 12 September 1980.

**Elif**   A coup in Turkey.

**Berker**   Another American ting?

**Elif**   It's terrible, killings, torture, imprisonment . . .

**Berker**   But it also gives Baba a new lease on life.

**Elif**   What?

**Berker**   A purpose.

**Elif**   He goes home to fight.

**Berker**   As naked as when he arrived ten years ago.

**Elif**   No. This time his case is full. Full of things for his family who he hadn't seen in over ten years. But also full of things of the family he won't see for many years. Full of pictures of his wife. And his son. Evidence of something, a life that could have been.

*Beat.* **Mustafa** *stands between them, holding the purple briefcase.*

**Janice**   So he decides to run away.

**Elif**   He's had enough of waiting and sitting around and feeling useless to the world. He's taking action –

**Berker**   Because he has nothing else to do.

**Elif**   You wouldn't get it.

**Berker**   Trust me, I've wanted to run away from my problems many times.

**Elif**   He feels a responsibility, to protect his country, to –

**Mustafa**   – to do something, I can't just watch as people are tortured, shot and left for dead. These are my people.

**Janice**   What about us? What about your son?

**Mustafa**   I have a responsibility.

**Janice**   You have a responsibility to your family.

**Mustafa**   And I'll come back. But I need this. I need to do this.

**Janice**   How do you think you'll come back? How is that going to work?

**Mustafa**   I'll find a way.

**Janice**   There's no way they'll let you back in!

**Mustafa**   I've always found a way.

**Janice**   You won't.

**Mustafa**   I don't have the right documents now but when I come back I will.

**Janice**   You'd really risk that?

**Mustafa**   I don't have a choice. I have to go.

**Janice**   So, just hypothetically, if you had the right documents, if you had a job, would you still leave?

**Mustafa**   I –

**Janice**   If you still owned the shop and you were allowed to stay here, if no one questioned you, would you still leave?

*Beat.*

**Mustafa**   My family should understand. My family should support me.

**Janice**   You're a coward.

**Mustafa**   I'm going to fight.

**Janice**   You're running away.

**Mustafa**   It's my duty. My responsibility. (*Addressing* **Berker**.) My son understands. He knows that I have a responsibility. Right?

*Beat.*

Right? He understands why I have to leave? For our people.

*Beat.*

He shares my values. Right? To fight for freedom, for democracy. Right?

*Beat.*

**Janice** *exits.* **Mustafa** *picks up some dirt from the garden and puts it in his pocket.*

**Mustafa**   Something to remember home.

*He walks off.* **Berker** *watches him.*

**Elif**   How old were you?

**Berker**   What? Oh. One and a half?

**Elif**   You remember this?

**Berker**   Well, you know with memory . . . is it real or am I remembering pictures or the stories my mum told me?

**Elif**   But you do.

**Berker**   I remember the way he smelled.

**Elif** *and* **Berker**   Kolonya!

**Berker**   Still?

**Elif**   Till the end.

**Berker**   Wow.

**Elif**   This is where you grew up? Just you and your mum.

**Berker**   Yeah.

**Elif**   She must hate Baba.

**Berker**   I don't think she thinks about him very much anymore.

**Elif**   She still lives here?

**Berker**   No.

**Elif**   Where is she?

**Berker**   She's . . . er –

**Elif**   Dead?

**Berker**   No! Nothing like that

**Elif**   Oh.

**Berker**   What?

**Elif**   . . . really?

**Berker**   What?

**Elif**   You English . . . I can't believe you.

**Berker**   What?!

**Elif**   This woman dedicates her life to you and you send her to a care home?

**Berker**   How did you know?

**Elif**   Oh I know that look.

**Berker**  Well, crucially, she can't have done it from her care home, can she?

**2023**

**Investigator One**  You should be ashamed of yourself.

**Berker**  What?

**Investigator One**  Your poor mother . . .

**Berker**  What does this have to do with anything?

**Investigator One**  You English . . .

**Investigator Two**  Your mother was never a serious suspect.

**Berker**  No.

**Investigator Two**  So what's your game, Mr Walker? Why are you taking us on this merry-go-round?

**Berker**  I'm answering your questions.

**Investigator Two**  Are you?

**Berker**  I am! Ask me anything.

**Investigator Two**  Where is your sister now?

**Berker**  I don't – I don't know.

**Investigator Two**  Why did you come to Turkey?

**Berker**  To reconnect with my baba.

**Investigator Two**  But why reconnect right at that moment? Nothing pushed you to do so?

**Berker**  I just – I don't know. I just felt I needed to.

**Investigator One** (*sarcastic*)  He doesn't know.

**Investigator Two**  Let's recap, shall we? You arrive at the hospital just at the moment that the body is being identified. In fact you claim to have happened to arrive in Turkey right after the death. You arrive and the first thing you do is impersonate an officer, which of course I could arrest you for right now –

**Berker**    I never pretended to be a Turkish police –

**Investigator Two**    But leaving that matter aside you then proceed to convince your grieving sister to start an investigation that looks at everyone but yourself.

**Berker**    I did a good job. I'm trying to walk you through the –

**Investigator One**    All you're doing is pointing at dead-ends.

**Berker**    Don't write that down. I did a good job.

**Investigator Two**    I don't have patience for your nonsense, Mr Walker. My boss's boss needs the arrests to be done yesterday. So I need the responsible party tonight.

**Investigator One**    Or did you focus your attention only on old women? Our careers depend on this, Mr Berker. We're not leaving without answers.

**Berker**    You're misunderstanding – I'm trying. Look we – we went through other suspects I can tell you about . . .

*As* **Berker** *explains, the characters appear and disappear, being interviewed by* **Elif***, like neo-noir vignettes. These should be theatrical, almost cartoonish.*

**Berker**    There was the neighbour with the haircut, who had accused Baba of stealing his cats and said that he'd kill him if he ever did again – that's a verbal threat! A verbal threat!

**Investigator Two**    We know about the neighbour. He has an alibi.

**Investigator One**    He was at the hairdresser at the time of the murder . . .

**Berker**   Yes. Yes. And then there was the ice cream man who Baba owed forty ice creams' worth! And he was going broke so he needed the money and he had –

**Investigator Two**   He had gone to see your father that day about the money. But then he was seen peddling imitation Häagen-Dazs on the side of the motorway the night of the murder.

**Berker**   And of course there was –

**Investigator Two**   We know about the Romanian horse jockey at the racecourse in Bursa and we know about the former communist comrade who wanted to build a luxury hotel on your land.

**Berker**   What about the French –

**Investigator One**   The French pornographic actor who was in love with your father and fell into a terrible rage when your father rejected his advances? Yes we've heard that story.

**Berker**   But do you –

**Investigator One**   And we know it is a rumour started by your father to tease the ladies at the mosque.

**Investigator Two**   We also know you arrived in Turkey three days before you claim you did.

**Berker**   What are you –

**Investigator Two**   It's time you stop wasting our time here, Mr Walker.

**Investigator One**   What did you do for three days?

**Berker**   I swear I was just sat in my hotel room eating room service. Chips and that. I was just nervous is all. I promise. You can check with the hotel.

**Investigator Two**   You said you investigated yourself. Tell us about that.

**Berker**   Well, if you already know all the –

**Investigator One**   We want to hear it from you.

**Investigator Two**   What was Elif's theory?

**Investigator One**   Why did you come to Turkey?

# _Option Three: Berker_

**2016**

**Berker**   Oh come off it.

**Elif**   There's motive.

**Berker**   I don't even know how to use a gun, how on earth would I have shot my own father?

**Elif**   That's convenient.

**Berker**   Can we please get serious again.

**Elif**   Need to explore all options don't we? Good detectives, detail-oriented.

**Berker**   Yeah but I wasn't even here.

**Elif**   So you say.

**Berker**   I can show you my boarding pass.

**Elif**   You're telling me that can't be faked?

**Berker**   I was in London yesterday! How could I have killed my father from London?

**Elif**   There's a lot of ways in which you can kill someone from across the world. When was the last time you saw Baba?

**Berker**   Do we have to do this?

**Elif**   The more you evade, the more suspicious you get.

**Berker**   Years ago. In London.

**Elif**   What happened?

**Berker**   We met at Paddington. He reached out. First and last time.

**Elif**   Paddington? Paddington Bear?

**Berker**   Train station. London.

**2008**

*Paddington.* **Mustafa** *enters, carrying a red briefcase.*

**Elif**    When was this?

**Berker**    Must be eight years now. He found me on Facebook.

**Mustafa**    Berker. I can't believe it's you.

**Berker**    See – I've got nothing to hide.

**Mustafa**    *Oğlum.*

**Berker**    Can you make him stop though.

**Mustafa**    My son. Come here.

**Berker**    I don't want this, Elif. This isn't how I remember –

**Elif**    Yes, it is.

**Mustafa**    Berker.

**Berker**    No this feels wrong.

**Elif**    It's your memory.

**Berker**    No, I don't –

**Mustafa**    I've missed you so much.

**Berker**    It's been twenty fucking years, YOU CAN'T HAVE MISSED ME THAT MUCH.

*Beat.*

**Mustafa**    I tried to find you. I thought I was coming back.

**Berker**    Yes. Well, here I am.

**Mustafa**    I brought you something.

*He hands* **Berker** *a bag of seeds.*

**Berker**    What is this?

**Mustafa**   Seeds from my garden. Japanese maple tree. You can plant them in your home and that way we –

**Berker**   What am I going to do with seeds?

**Mustafa**   Plant them and watch a tree –

**Berker**   Whatever, thanks. Did you also bring what I asked you for?

**Mustafa**   Can we catch up. Maybe grab a coffee or?

**Berker**   I asked you for something. Did you bring it?

**Mustafa**   Hey, do you still watch that show with the bananas –

**Berker**   I was a baby when you left.

**Mustafa**   So grown-up now. *Oğlum. Nasıl sin?*

**Berker**   I don't speak Turkish.

**Mustafa**   She didn't –

**Berker**   Why did you want to meet?

**Mustafa**   You know I went to prison?

**Berker**   I'm sorry that happened to you, Mustafa.

**Mustafa**   Call me Baba.

**Berker**   No thanks.

**Mustafa**   Berker . . . we're still family. I still love you.

**Berker**   Take some responsibility! We're not family.

**Mustafa**   I thought I was coming back. I wanted to be there. I wanted –

**Berker**   No one forced you to go.

**Mustafa**   1980 it was . . . my friends were being shot in the street. I had to do *something*. Being part of a culture, a community, it means taking responsibility. Sacrifice.

You work for it. You earn it.

**Berker**   Responsibility. Ha.

**Mustafa**   Yes, responsibility.

**Berker**   What about leaving a toddler fatherless screams responsible behaviour for you? What about your responsibility for me?

**Mustafa**   All of it, everything I do, is for you. I went for you! For you to have a future. To fight for a world in which you can live. For you. *Oğlum.*

**Berker**   Why did you want to meet?

**Mustafa**   You wanted to connect to your heritage right, learn about Turkey? I can help with that.

**Berker**   All I'm doing is applying for citizenship. That's all.

**Mustafa**   Exactly. So I thought we could together –

**Berker**   I don't need anything from you.

**Mustafa**   You need my birth certificate.

*Beat.*

You feel lost, you've felt lost haven't you?

**Berker**   I –

**Mustafa**   Who are you?

**Berker**   I'm me.

**Mustafa**   And who is that?

**Berker**   I don't need to justify that to you.

**Mustafa**   Why are you applying for citizenship?

**Berker**   I just, ugh! I just thought it might help me . . . belong somewhere.

**Mustafa**   Do you not feel like you belong anywhere?

**Berker**   Just . . . I. It doesn't matter. Do you have it?

**Mustafa**   Who are you?

**Berker**   Who are *you*?

**Mustafa**   I'm your baba.

*Beat.*

See, soon Turkey will be joining the EU and then I can visit you whenever –

**Berker**   When have you tried to visit me?

**Mustafa**   I've been doing my research. By 2011 at the latest. But for now it's difficult.

**Berker**   Where have you heard that?

**Mustafa**   See, I brought these documents for you to sign –

**Berker**   Documents?

**Mustafa**   All you need to do is sign and it'll make everything simple.

**Berker**   What are you talking about?

**Mustafa**   I want to come back to London. With your mother sick you need someone. I want to be there for you.

**Berker**   Don't you have a family in Turkey? Don't you have a kid?

**Mustafa**   Nothing to worry about.

**Berker**   How can you say that? I know that you –

**Mustafa**   These documents prove that we're related. That you're my son. And so you can apply for citizenship and I can –

**Berker**   The only reason you wanted to see me is to come back to the UK.

**Mustafa**   No. I wanted to see you.

**Berker**   Bullshit.

**Mustafa**   Berker, it's just a signature, it can help us both. All it does is prove that I'm your –

**Berker**   But you're not my dad are you? I don't want to see you anymore.

**Mustafa**   Please. *Oğlum.*

**Berker**   I'm sorry I can't do this.

**Mustafa**   *Oğlum.*

*He stays stood despondent as* **Berker** *returns to 2016.*

**Elif**   I thought you came here to reconnect with him?

**Berker**   I did.

**Elif**   But the last time you saw him you rejected his attempt at doing just that.

**Berker**   I wasn't . . . I wasn't ready.

**Elif**   Why did you come here?

**Berker**   I told you.

**Elif**   It's just a coincidence that the man you have come to 'reconnect' with turns up dead the same day?

**Berker**   I mean . . . yes. It is. Granted a big coincidence. But. Come on you don't seriously think . . .

**Elif**   Why are you here?

**Berker**   I think – I

**Elif**   Are you really a police officer?

**Berker**   I . . . what?

**Elif**   Tell me the truth.

**Berker**   What are you talking about?

**Elif**    Please . . . a police officer who doesn't immediately go to the police?

**Berker**    I –

**Elif**    Are you a police officer?

**Berker**    . . . no.

**Elif**    Truth, finally. What is your actual job?

**Berker**    I uhm . . . I . . . it's boring.

**Elif**    What?

**Berker**    I work for a toy company.

**Elif**    Toys?

**Berker**    Yeah but I just like . . . I do data entry.

**Elif**    Kids' data?

**Berker**    Also if we're . . . being honest now . . . I also lost my job.

**Elif**    Aha! So no money, no prospects, stick Mama in a care home and then come to Turkey to get your inheritance. Is that it?

**Berker**    No that's not –

**Umut** *enters in uniform.*

**Umut**    Elif, they are here.

**Berker**    Who's this?

**Umut**    Oh! Hello. I am Umut, fiancé of the Elif.

**Berker**    No way.

**Umut**    You are Berker?

**Berker**    Are you an actor she hired? You hired an actor didn't you? He's an actor. People are not this hot in real life. And that uniform . . .

**Umut**    Nice to meet! I practise English for England.

**Berker**    For England?

**Umut**    We go to England! For me.

**Berker**    For you?

**Umut**    Elif, the people are here for the house.

**Elif**    My love I don't know what to do.

**Umut**    It will be okay. You made the right decision. You've got this.

**Elif**    I'm just so tired.

**Umut**    It will be over soon.

*They hug.*

**Berker**    What did he say?

**Elif**    Nothing.

**Umut**    People buying for house.

**Berker**    Already? Elif, he's not even in the –

**Elif**    Just let me. I'll be one minute we just –

**Berker**    Come on!

**Elif** *and* **Umut** *leave.* **Berker***'s not quite sure what to do with himself. He watches the 'memory' of* **Mustafa** *tending to the garden. Eventually, he goes to watch close-up.*

**Mustafa**    The crocuses are finally blooming. Sometimes I just like to sit and look at the purple.

*Beat.*

Don't you agree, Berker?

**Berker**    What?

**Mustafa**    Don't you love crocuses?

**Berker**    Erm . . . what's happening.

**Mustafa**   Crocuses are the purple ones.

**Berker**   How are you . . . this isn't how it works. You're –

**Mustafa**   I asked you if you liked crocuses, can't you listen?

**Berker**   Yeah . . . they're pretty.

**Mustafa**   My favourite, though, is that Japanese maple tree in autumn. When the leaves fall, and the ground is flooded with rich reds. Nothing compares to that red.

**Berker**   Uh-huh.

**Mustafa**   A healthy garden is about taking care of the soil, not the plants.

**Berker**   Okay?

**Mustafa**   I need you to do something for me.

**Berker**   You're dead?

**Mustafa**   I'm still your baba.

**Berker**   Okay . . .

**Mustafa**   I need you to find who killed me.

**Berker**   I've been trying! I –

**Mustafa**   No more fucking about. You want me to rest in peace? Find who killed me. Point the finger.

**Berker**   Wait – can you tell me? Surely you know who shot you.

**Mustafa**   That's not how this works. I'm sorry.

**Berker**   But –

**Mustafa**   Stop messing around with history. What happened yesterday?

**Berker**   The stuff. The military stuff?

**Mustafa**   What kind of stuff?

**Berker**    The coup stuff. Oh my God . . . he's a soldier.

**Mustafa**    Good.

**Berker**    Of course. The soldier. The coup. It was right there
. . . Thanks, Dad.

**Mustafa**    For fuck's sake, call me Baba.

*He leaves.*

**Berker**    Wait. Dad. Baba. Wait. What happened yesterday?

**Elif** *enters with* **Bahriye**.

**Elif**    They'll come back later. But my mum is here so –

**Bahriye**    Hello, Berker.

**Berker**    What happened yesterday, Elif?

**Elif**    What do you mean?

**Bahriye**    What's he saying?

**Elif**    One second mum.

**Berker**    What was your boyfriend doing yesterday?

**Elif**    He was . . . he was working.

**Bahriye**    Yes.

**Berker**    I'm sorry, Elif.

**Elif**    What?

## _Option Four: Elif's Boyfriend_

**Elif**  I beg you be mature.

**Berker**  Your boyfriend is a soldier! Our dad was shot the night of a military insurrection.

**Elif**  . . . so?

**Berker**  Yeah. Exactly.

**Elif**  What do you want?

**Berker**  Last night. What happened?

**Elif**  You're the suspect! Not Umut.

**Berker**  What was it about having nothing to hide, nothing to fear?

**Elif**  You've come here, and you're just twisting it all around to fit your version . . . I knew I shouldn't trust you.

**Berker**  Tell the story, Elif.

**Elif**  I don't want to.

**Berker** _gets out his phone. He starts reading. The night of the coup._

**Berker**  Last night a faction of the military tried to overthrow the government. They bombed parliament with fighter jets and they tried to kill President Erdogan.

**Elif**  Where are you reading this?

**Berker**  Reddit. Typical for a coup the army starts taking over civilian buildings. Showing their presence on the street. But – for the first time in this country's history the public resisted. Everyday citizens stood in the way of the tanks and the guns and said: No!

**Umut** _enters carrying a gun._

**Berker**  And Umut surely would have been working.

**Elif**  It's not –

**Berker**    Which side are you on?

**Elif**    I'm . . . I don't . . . Why do I have to have a side?

**Berker**    Everyone has a side.

**Elif**    I don't know.

**Bahriye**    I know.

**Elif**    Stay out of it!

**Bahriye**    Grow up.

*She whispers to her phone. An English translation is loudly audible, maybe in her voice.*

Like with all war, or revolution, what is most striking is the absurdity of it all for those on the ground. Because if you're say an everyday foot soldier from a rural part of the country, what happens is you find yourself pointing your gun at your neighbour, your doctor, your teacher, your cab driver, your friend, your lover . . . or their dad.

**Mustafa** *enters carrying a pot and wooden spoon.*

**Bahriye**    And you're screaming:

**Umut**    FREEDOM! Stand down. I'm here to give you freedom!

**Elif**    He was hardly –

**Bahriye**    After the first brave civilians take to the streets, quickly many follow, armed only with pots and pans and that most overwhelming sensation: solidarity.

**Mustafa** *faces off with* **Umut**. **Elif** *leaves.*

**Bahriye**    Like many others Mustafa went out that night. As meaningless as the word can be – he would always prefer democracy to military rule.

*More civilians arrive holding pots and pans. They start banging their utensils. They encircle* **Umut**. *He looks terrified.*

**Bahriye**   And while in Istanbul and Ankara the big battles are being fought – the famous moments of tanks on the Galata bridge, or the officers who defied orders and protected MPs at the National Assembly – no one was really looking at the small towns. No one was really, in a serious way paying attention to places like Küçükköy. So, in the early hours of the morning when in Istanbul, in Ankara, in all the big cities the outcome is already clear, when soldiers are being told to stand down, when the generals have been detained, in Küçükköy a small squadron, whose phone batteries long ago died, are still surrounded by the clanking of pots and the ringing of pans. And chain of command, well, what does that mean in the fog of war?

*Chaos. The civilians charge* **Umut**. *It's all a jangle of limbs until –*

*A gunshot.*

*The civilians disperse. All we see is* **Umut** *and a body crumpled on the ground.*

**Berker**   I knew it.

**Umut**   Wait! Berker you is policeman in England?

**Berker**   I – uhm – sort of.

**Umut**   I have visa for England.

**Berker**   You – what?

**Umut**   I leave tomorrow. I must tell you truth. I have never shoot my gun. Very scared. I don't follow order.

*The scene repeats. The civilians return. This time we see it play out more clearly.* **Umut** *points his gun, but terrified, lowers it.*

*Suddenly – a gunshot.*

*He looks behind him:* **Elif**, *in uniform, holding the smoking gun.*

*Then, the body:* **Mustafa**, *unconscious.*

**Berker**   Elif?

**Elif**　Baba!

*She runs to her dad's aid.* **Umut** *runs away.*

**Elif**　Help! Help! Someone help! I'm so sorry. Baba. I didn't see you. Baba. Baba . . .

*The civilians rush back.* **Elif** *tries to pick up her dad. The civilians help her carry him. They lay him down on a hospital bed.*

**Berker**　It was you?

**Elif**　Baba . . . .Baba . . . .

**Berker**　You?

**Elif**　Oh my baba . . .

## Option Five: Elif

**Elif**   You don't understand anything, Berker.

**Berker**   You killed him. You killed him for some vague political cause you hardly believe in yourself.

**Elif**   That version gives us nothing.

**Berker**   Elif, I saw you. This is absurd. You killed him.

**Elif**   Of course it is absurd! It has to be. You just can't understand. You know the facts and the figures but what you can never grasp, what you English can never understand is that from here, from where I stand the world doesn't make sense. How do you make sense of all this? You can't reason or rationalise your way out of it. Trying to understand the way you look at the world . . . it will just not add up.

**Berker**   It's not that complicated: You killed him and now you're selling his house to leave with your boyfriend.

**Elif**   You're going to blame every soldier who followed orders?

**Berker**   You are responsible for what you –

*The stage transforms. We are back at the night of the coup. Same staging, but instead of* **Elif** *there is faceless person wearing her uniform.* **Mustafa** *charges, the person lifts their gun. It all freezes.*

**Elif**   We were ordered to shoot at anyone threatening us. I would have been court martialled if I didn't. If the coup had succeeded I could be in prison or worse. So was it me or the uniform?

**Mustafa** *is shot by the faceless uniform. Everyone flees.*

**Berker**   You didn't have to pull the trigger.

**Elif**   The trigger? The gun I was using was designed by a Swiss company, manufactured in Germany, and imported to

Turkey who were hoping the purchase would help EU accession.

*The same tableau, but instead of the faceless uniform, the gun is floating in mid-air.*

**Elif**   Did the gun manufacturer kill Baba? It was a rubber bullet. We were only just issued these guns and they are significantly more powerful than manufacturer claims. Very different to the previous issue.

**Berker**   A rubber bullet from, like, 10 feet will kill an old man.

**Elif**   Not necessarily. But maybe a sick old man.

**Mustafa** *is shot by the floating gun. Everyone flees.*

**Berker**   What?

**Elif**   Baba had lung and heart problems largely due to the large volume of plastic burned in our area.

**Berker**   Plastic?

**Elif**   The EU ships their plastic recycling to us but most of it just gets burned in huge piles. We get plumes of smoke coming here every few weeks. Baba's lungs were coal-black. Did the EU kill him? If the plastic wasn't burnt in our area his body might have been able to survive the rubber bullet.

**Berker**   You're claiming the EU killed my dad with plastic rubbish?

**Elif**   You don't understand anything.

**Berker**   I understand that you killed him and now you're selling the house so you and your boyfriend can live it up in London.

**Elif**   You don't even know him.

**Berker**   Umut? Yeah I don't want to –

**Elif**  Baba! You've met him once in your adult life! What is it you think you will get out of this?

**Berker**  He's my dad. My baba. I know.

**Elif**  You – fuck it.

*The scene transforms.* **Elif**'*s memory.* **Mustafa** *enters.*

**Mustafa**  Oh look who's showed up. To what do I owe this pleasure?

**Elif**  Fuck.

**Berker**  What is this?

**Elif**  The last time *I* saw Baba.

**Mustafa**  Let me look at you.

**Elif**  Baba.

**Mustafa**  So grown-up. Wow.

**Elif**  It's good to see you.

**Mustafa**  If you enjoy it so much maybe try coming more than every five years.

**Elif**  I wanted to see you to –

**Mustafa**  You've joined the military.

**Elif**  I . . . yes.

**Mustafa**  You look good in uniform.

**Elif**  That's not what why I –

**Mustafa**  You've always enjoyed authority roles. I remember when you were little you loved bossing the other kids around the playground. Captain of the football team. You were great to watch on the pitch. Commandeering.

**Elif**  Sure.

**Mustafa**  What – you don't believe me? I know things. I know things about you that you don't know. I know.

**Elif**   Do you want me to get you some water?

**Mustafa**   I'm not thirsty.

**Elif**   Have you even eaten anything today?

**Mustafa**   You're just like your mother.

**Elif**   You need to take care of yourself.

**Mustafa**   You blame me. Wow. She's really done a number on you, eh. You blame me.

**Elif**   I don't want to get into this.

**Mustafa**   She left me. She took you away from me.

**Elif**   It's complicated.

**Mustafa**   She left me for no reason and she took you away and so I'm sorry if I don't know when you stopped playing football.

**Elif**   Seven.

**Mustafa**   Seven years ago? Well, there you go. Not too shabby.

**Elif**   No, I was seven.

**Mustafa**   If she hadn't taken you away from me, then –

**Elif**   We really don't have to do this every time. You could have come to see me.

**Mustafa**   So the new boyfriend is behind all this?

**Elif**   The – what? What are you talking about

**Mustafa**   I guess your mother was always a bit of a whore.

**Elif**   What?

**Mustafa**   Apple doesn't fall far from the – I tried. God knows I did. You can't blame me for being a fucking idiot.

**Elif**   I don't even – how – can you not talk in that way. You're being horrible.

**Mustafa**    Hey, I've got something interesting to show you. I've been doing some research.

*Newspaper clippings.* **Mustafa** *takes them out, chaotically, creating a mess. He's hanging some of them up on the pin board as he speaks.*

**Mustafa**    Those guns you're using at work are imported from the EU. Some of the sharpest analysts think that we're buying them as part of sweetener to join. They are announcing it in the next year.

**Elif**    Okay, Baba.

**Mustafa**    What – you don't believe me? Look for yourself. I've got every British, German and French article of the past decade here. It's all in black and white.

**Elif**    Do you even speak German?

**Mustafa**    Mr Google does.

**Elif**    The garden is looking a little worse for wear, Baba.

**Mustafa**    2011: 'Turkey's chances of accession receive a significant boost' – BBC News.

**Elif**    I can come by more often and help with the garden.

**Mustafa**    2013: 'Will Turkey ever join the EU? Yes' – *BILD* magazine.

**Elif**    You're taking care of yourself aren't you?

**Mustafa**    Me? I'm fine. I'm fine. It's your mother you should worry about. You do know why she left us?

**Elif**    She didn't leave me.

**Mustafa**    Typical of your mother. She can never look past the past. You see? You need to look past the past. Oh – this is a good one. 2010: 'Turkey is the dream candidate. A leader in European values. what are we waiting for?' – *Private Eye* magazine.

**Elif**   I think that's a satirical – whatever. Baba. I wanted to talk to you about something.

**Mustafa**   2013: 'Is Turkey still a viable candidate? Probably' – *Le Monde*.

**Elif**   Baba, soon certain events will take place and when they do I want you to please stay at home.

**Mustafa**   You see I've been following this all very closely. In this country we sit around and watch as they smack us across the face time and again. And what do we do? We turn the other cheek. Why? Well. Well. Look at this.

*He gets out a picture of the EU flag superimposed on an alien lizard.*

Do you see?

**Elif**   Baba . . .

**Mustafa**   The world is controlled by a shady cabal of shapeshifting lizard people. The EU is run by alien lizards. It's all in the documents. They haven't even bothered properly hiding. You just have to look it up. They put on human skin costumes and go out and pretend to be politicians . . . Their goal is to divide us, to enslave us. Of course none of what's going on makes sense. Of course the cruelty is senseless. Our job now is to make sure the world knows. Because if people know – there is power in that. Like in 1980 when I fought against those military bastards – we just needed people to understand. And it's working. I have made a Facebook page, it already has 312 likes! Elif! 312 people just from me. This is the start of a revolution. Do you hear?

**Elif**   Baba, please listen to me. I don't have details. I'm going off whispers, but pretty solid whispers. The army, or most of the army, we are planning to, well, I'm not, I'm just hearing whispers that there are plans of a . . . democratic intervention.

**Mustafa**    A what?

**Elif**    Restoring our country's values. Taking back control from this government. Bringing back the values that we – European values. Western values. There's also whispers of an American connection. It's a good thing. For us. Our future.

**Mustafa**    A coup?

**Elif**    I think we prefer not to . . . not to call it that.

**Mustafa**    It's getting late.

**Elif**    Baba, please.

**Mustafa**    I'm tired, my love. You go home now. Go home now and get some rest.

**Elif**    Baba, please stay at home. Please. Just promise me that. Baba.

**Mustafa**    My love, the day we stop fighting is the day the lizards win.


**2023**

**Investigator Two**    Be clear, Mr Walker.

**Investigator One**    Who shot your father?

**Berker**    The funeral.

**Investigator Two**    What?

**Berker**    It becomes clear at the funeral.


**2016**

**Berker**    Oh. Hello. Hi. *Merhaba*. Yes, Berker. Me. Berker. Hello.

**Elif**    Thank you, everyone, for coming. My baba was a . . . complicated man, and in his unusual way he wanted something unusual for his funeral. He's requested his ashes be scattered in his favourite place on Earth: our garden. Let him grow into a strong tree.

*She spreads the ashes.*

**Elif**   That's all. Thanks.

**Berker** *stands.*

**Berker**   I would like to say some words –

**Elif**   Berker!

**Berker**   I just wanted to speak for a moment. In my culture we usually give speeches at funerals.

*An* **Alien Lizard** *enters the scene, watching.* **Berker** *notices but doesn't address it.*

**Berker**   Who do you blame? The woman, the gun, or politics?

I came all this way to see my dad die, if we're being real, I came to see him die, but all I got was a lollipop. It didn't even taste nice, but that doctor's kindness gave me more comfort and care than my dad could bother with his entire life. She didn't even know me. I'm your son. When Mum got sick I lived with Uncle Stephen for a year. Uncle fucking Stephen who smells like rancid tomato juice and foot cream.

The woman, the gun or politics.

I'm sorry, Elif. I don't understand you or your . . . I just wanted to . . . Wanted to feel . . .

I didn't even need him to be there.

I didn't need you I just needed to know you cared.

The worst bit is that I don't understand why I care so much.

Why do I care? I don't even like you.

The worst bit is it could have been so much better and now it never will be. Because as much as you hate yourself for admitting it, while they are still alive, a small part of you still holds onto the brainworms idea that it will get better that if only one of you did or said one thing to make it so, that it would happen. And now it won't. Now you're dead. And I don't even know who to blame.

Alien lizards?


**2023**

**Investigator Two**    Mr Walker, this is a serious investigation.

**Berker**    Lizards they come from outer space, yeah, and they put on human costumes and they say things like, 'I'm Rishi Sunak', but really, if you listen, if you listen closely, you can hear them going 'ssssssssss'.

**Investigator One**    Mr Berker!

**Berker**    Look at it. It all makes sense. It all fits together. Your problem is you've gone about this the wrong way. In a situation like this you can't try and find a culprit. You can't point a finger. Unless you realise – alien lizards.

*He moves to the board, connecting the various bits of information as he speaks.*

**Berker**    Alien lizards caused my baba to move to England in the seventies because of the political problems in Turkey. They stopped him from being able to get papers, they dressed up as 'Thatcher', they overthrew the Turkish government in 1980, they confused him, drew him to all sides, they imprisoned him, they freed him, they are the EU, they made him obsessed with the EU, they made him lose his family, both, lose everything, they made another coup in 2016, they made him take to the streets, they made the coup fail, they let people die, Earthquakes and war and recycling and – and – and now my dad is dead. It's all crystal clear, the EU are alien lizards and they killed my dad, don't you see?

**Investigator Two**   You are making yourself a prime suspect, Mr Walker. A prime suspect for this investigation.

**Berker**   I'm pointing at the prime suspect, but you won't listen to me! Unless you work for them? Do you?

**Investigator One**   Behave yourself!

**Investigator Two**   Where is your sister? Where is Elif?

**Berker**   I've already told you. I don't know.

**Investigator One**   All day you've only told us stuff we already know.

**Investigator Two**   Stop playing games.

**Berker**   Do you see this tree there – that red maple? Isn't it beautiful? I planted that seven years ago and look how it's grown. It's not native to this part of the world but here it has prospered. You know why? Because to start a garden you need to take care of the roots. You don't give it too much water, you try and make it find its own water source. So that's how a tree that's not even a decade old is this beautiful, strong.

**Investigator Two**   What are you talking about?

**Berker**   You said you wanted to hear something you didn't already know. I bet you didn't know that.

**Investigator One**   You are pissing me off.

**Berker**   I've answered your questions truthfully. If you don't like my version, just go and find someone else who tells you what you want to hear. That's how this works, isn't it?

**Investigator One**   We could arrest you right now.

**Investigator Two**   We just need to point the finger. That's how this works.

**Berker**   But you won't. Because I'm a British citizen and without hard evidence that would mean a lot of faff for your superiors, which means a lot of faff for you. That's the elephant in the room isn't it? That's how this works.

**Investigator Two**    This isn't the last you're hearing of us.

*The* **Investigators** *leave.* **Berker** *is alone with the tree and the* **Alien Lizard**.

**2016**

**Elif**   Hello?

**Berker** *enters, carrying gardening equipment.*

**Berker**   I didn't think you'd come.

**Elif**   July 16.

**Berker**   Seven years. I can't believe it. Time just . . . I'm glad you came.

**Elif**   Wouldn't miss a year.

**Berker**   Shall we?

**Elif** *gets out a bag of seeds.*

**Elif**   Guava.

**Berker**   Guava?

**Elif**   About time this garden bore some fruit. Gardens aren't just for show, you know.

**Berker**   And which part of the world did you bring these from?

**Elif** *plants the seeds.*

**Elif**   For you, Baba.

**Berker** *assists her.*

*A moment for their ritual.*

*And then it's over.*

**Elif**   Garden looks good. I didn't think the maple tree would last in this heat.

**Berker** *shrugs.*

**Berker**   Police came by yesterday. Asking about Baba.

**Elif**   And?

**Berker**    Cold case. All the perpetrators to be brought to justice.

**Elif**    I see.

*Beat.*

**Berker**    What should we do?

**Elif**    What do you mean?

**Berker**    Shouldn't we do something? Aren't you worried? They want answers.

**Elif**    What did you tell them?

**Berker**    The police? I just – a story. I told them a story.

**Elif**    What else is there to do?

Printed in the USA
CPSIA information can be obtained
at www.ICGtesting.com
LVHW021247160624
783255LV00009B/326